AF484746

Poems by Tracey Lapham White and Jason White
Book layout Tracey Lapham White
Cover design Jason White
Published by HG Publishing

First Live Edition, 2022

LIVE

Cool Summer Nights Edition

Tracey Lapham White

Jason White

Summer is kicked off by the solstice. It holds great beauty and intensity. The heat combined with the swift pace of life can leave you feeling out of breath and thirsty. Each season – indeed, everything related to Mother Earth – has specific attributes, gifts, and lessons that are rich and complex. They require living… which is assuredly the essence of summer. Everything is amplified. Life is busy with growing and expanding. We, too, are growing; in awareness, experience, and understanding. Most of us find ourselves busy. We are out in Nature, spending time with family and friends, taking advantage of longer days, and we pack them full. Relationships are one of the prominent features. Summer is the seat of the fire. It can be destructive if given free rein; however, it also transforms. In the Summer we are reminded to have Faith, Trust, and Humility; you need each to learn to work with the fire. Summer months find us listening to the storms caused by the heat of the days, and the cooling of the nights when the Thunderbird is reborn.

Flowers bloom
Fields of buttercups sprout
Aromas collide,
Painting the picture of pure beauty

We lay in the tall grass
Kissing each other
Moving in perfect harmony
The buttercups painting our skin

The color of happiness
Sun's warmth
Our hearts feel complete

It rains
Nothing washes away,
But the air feels
Clearer
Petrichor, it's called, yes?
I can smell it,
But I could never use words to describe it
I'd have to invite you over

The summer harvest
Brings gorgeous memories
Our plates are full
Of Mother's bounty
We feast
Then light the fires
We drink and laugh
And build our memories

LIVE

Cool Summer Nights Edition

We are all brothers and sisters
Yet we war
Based on ignorance

Perhaps
We don't truly understand
Our skin and language mean
Less to the conflicts of the past
Than we wish to think

Now, perhaps we refuse to understand
The conflicts of days long past
Are more an account
Of splintered family principles

Perhaps
It's time to understand
That we're all brothers and sisters

We chop the logs
Our brothers work their 9 - 5
We light the fire
We clean the fish and birds
Our sisters go to the grocery store
We are all working

Our grandparents sing the old songs
We turn on the radio
Our fathers beat the drum
We take guitar lessons from the guy down the
street
Our aunties tell the stories
We listen to audiobooks in the car on the way to
work
We are all artists

You turn the a/c up a few degrees
They weave new garments for our children
You wash our bedsheets once a week
They invite me to sleep under the stars
You put the spiders outside for me
They leave them be
We are all keeping house

Remember
Both sides of the track
Lead to the same place

Sometimes,
Something we wouldn't normally choose
Lands in our lives
Loves us
And shows us
That opposites attract

The fires rage
Warding off the chill of the night
We gather 'round
To tell stories
Some of glory
Some of fright
We let our imaginations take flight
The blankets come out
The fire gets fed
These are times that fill our heads
With love and laughter and good times
These are the greatest moments
Of our lives

In a dream
We rush to the river,
Hand in hand
Sweaty palms never losing contact
Eyes, wild
Lips, ready
For strawberries
For rain
A kiss

At the stream
We laugh until our sides hurt,
Splashing
Sandwiches eaten well before noon
Bellies, full
Foreheads, sweaty
Skinny dipping
Just us and the fish

Don't you just feel so

...

Full

I look out my window
What a beautiful day
The clouds are forming pictures
Telling me stories
I see a heart, brave
A bunny, so innocent
I see an elephant, playing
I watch in wonderment
As those pictures fade
And new pictures form
A mountain lion, stalking its prey
And a pair of stallions, running

It is mid-summer
The festival of Aphrodisia begins
The aroma of sweat
Is how we find our mate
If only for the night
A warm body to snuggle into
As the day cools to night
These days
We don't have to fight our demons
They're just simply too busy
Being in love
Like the rest of us

Dancing

Sunlight,
Moonlight,
It's all the same to us
Once the rhythm takes over

Drums beat,
Flames lick
Our sun-cooked arms,
Marshmallows,
Hot dogs

Eating, laughing
Til our bellies ache
Tears streaming,
Red face

You bring out the fun in me
You bring out the best in me

When inspiration strikes

It's usually because
The sun broke through grey skies

Laughter erupted from the children playing
outside
An old couple showed each other love

When inspiration strikes
It's usually because
The birds sang my favorite song
I saw a baby and all the hope they bring

When inspiration strikes
It's because she smiled at me

I can't just wait
        For inspiration
    It strikes so rarely

Inspiration prefers to sunbathe
    Illuminated in magical rays

            Energy seems unreachable
The gold pot at the ever-moving
        end of the rainbow
But when you get there, you just
                    Pick it up

            I find inspiration
    In a cup of coffee
A rickety chair on your porch,
        A smile in the eyes of a child
A drop of dew on a blade of grass
        (Small enough for me to forget)
        (Large enough to feast an ant)
I mustn't forget

I can't just wait, or hope
    I show up
        I move

        I inspire

Summer rain
Washes down my face
Warming my soul
And taking me to new places

It's a magical ride,
This sun,
This tide

A whole new world,
My eyes focus
My soul sees clearly

We are love

Summer rain
Washes a smile unto my face
Warming my heart
And giving me a new perspective on life

Maybe you didn't know,
But I see you
And it's okay
You are okay

We can be
Together
Apart
We can be okay

I trust me
You trust you
And we trust we
It's all okay

Rain washes
Everything away
That we no longer need
I'tll be okay

Rain gave life
To our bodies
And cleansed our souls
We have always been okay

I see you
You see me

Summer rain
Reminds me of what I have
Opening my eyes
To the blessings in my life

Close your eyes
Breathe in
Look around

See me seeing you

Don't you just feel so

...

Full

We run free
Frolicking in the sand
The chill of the lake
Is a most welcoming sensation
On this hot, sunny day

The laughter is a medicine
For our souls
Forgiveness of Winter's
Frost-bitten days, long past

Now we live in the moment

We live to run free
On those perfect Summer days

It was a Summer of love
A Summer I will never forget
It was a Summer of passion
A Summer of spiritual bliss

Our Summer of love
Will be ours for an eternity

Nothing is forever, they say
Maybe, but today
Will last forever in our hearts
And, every time I dream,
I'll bring us back here,
To celebrate simply being alive

I wrap my arms around you
Your smile brings me comfort
Perfection is all I see
It is everything I feel
When I wrap my arms around you

Fortune has certainly favored me
For when I look into your eyes
I hear a thousand Angels sing

Your heart has given mine
A reason to beat again

The purest of my memories
Collect in my mind
Like I would collect concert tickets
Or lockets of hair in a fancy book
Forty-five years of memories
Some so amazing
They take my breath away
Many of them come from my August days
That's forty-five Augusts
Shaping my heaven

Collect me like dog-ears, love

Favourite quotes in favourite books
Leave notes in my margins,
Reread my passages
until you know them by heart
Yellow highlighter,
scribbled questions

Collect me like dew drops, love

Wet denim from sitting in the field
See the rays of light I reflect,
Relish in my colours
Too many
or the human eye to comprehend
Green grass, blue skies

She says
Come with me
Come run

We'll run wild and free
The Summer breeze will kiss our faces
And the sands will take care of our feet
As we allow ourselves to fall into the ocean
Everybody else will fall away
Only we will remain

The world will become ours
For the moments our eyes connect

She says
We'll run wild and free
And I trust her
I leave the comfort of my home
These days belong to
Me and Her

These days
Blend into evenings,
Warm nights into birdsong

                    These days,
              It's hard to tell who's who
                We all blend together
                  In laughter and song

These days,
I forget the word for heartache
I only know here and now
Me, and you
An us that feels
Unbreakable

                    These days,
              The tears are of joy, only,
              Beautiful mist in our eyes,
          To thank the sun for another day
          To thank the moon for another night

These days
Blend together
Summer seems
A fever dream,
As they say

                    These nights
              I dream only of running
                And I fall, laughing,
              Breathless in your arms

The campfire is a sacred place
Why else would we form a circle
It's a place to share
A place for us to laugh
Or tell stories
It's a place for long moments of silence
And thought-provoking stares
The campfire is a place
To fall in love with each other again

The stage is set
We put our lawn chairs out
I am with the woman
I was supposed to love forever
And the man
I was never meant to know again
I hold her hand in mine
And I look over at him
She holds my hand a little tighter
And he gives me his signature crooked grin
As the band takes the stage

I wish for this night to never end

Let's build castles in the sky
Where our dreams can feel alive
Let's forge new opportunities
For our dreams to thrive

Let's build a home by the sea
So we can watch
As the world turns
For us and our dreams

Let's take an apartment in the city
Where the views are amazing
And the people are following their dreams

Sure, I should have seen you coming / from a mile away // Long hair, deep eyes, cool shirt, hips sway // You thought I was someone else // I knew there was no one like you // You asked if I'd like to go out // I didn't know what to do

Didn't know what I was missing / 'til you looked my way // Tattoos, no shoes, you smile, say "hey" // It all came so naturally to you // I was out of my element from the start // It all comes so easily to you // My heart was yours from the start

Never knew how to surf
But babe, I want to ride this wave
Of course we don't know where things will go
But maybe that's the fun of it?
I can't tear my thoughts away from you
Can't stop thinking what we could make together
Your beauty, my strength
The fierceness in your eyes,
The mouth on me
We make a great team
Why not make this more than a summer fling?

We could feel so alive
if only we could see through
our own eyes.

We could feel so alive
if only our eyes
weren't wide shut.

If we learned how to touch
ourselves
like we touch each other.

We could feel so alive.

Remember when you could
Smell the wind as it came up the hill?
It announced its presence
Warm   Inviting
Carrying scents in its pockets
Mint and oregano   Sage, too
And we kept the fires low
So we could cook our fish on coals

Remember when you could
Hear the tinkering from every house?
Neighbours shared their tools
Tips   Tricks
Bringing leftovers to eat in the garage
Covered in paint   Sawdust
And we kept our voices low
So the grownups didn't know what we were up to

Remember when you could
Feel the music in the Earth's very breath?
It danced through all the houses,
Trembling with   Gratitude
Holding power in its sturdiness
Anticipation and abundance
Calm, too
And we made the fires last long
So we could sing and dance together

The sky looks blue, because
It absorbs every hue of light
Except for blue

Blue rays
Ricochet
From somewhere in our atmosphere,
Until
We're all convinced we know
The nature of the sky,
Kilometres above us

I forgot how brightly I could shine

By the time I walked away,
You were
Bioluminescent

Follow the path
To brighter days
Allow me one more night
Of endless love

As warm sunny days come to a close
And greyer, cooler days fall upon us
We still carry the flame within
Our spirits, still playful
Our eyes, still full of hope
We still cling to our short and lighter clothes
We are not in denial
Of the changing seasons,
We are simply in love

It's okay,
Let go,
I'll see you again.

It all goes

'Round
    and
        'round.

lives in Barrie, Ontario, Canada doing what they love most: reading, writing, films, cleaning the house, making it messy again, good food, laughter, and education.
Tracey has a nine-year-old child, Jamie, who is full of insight, creativity, and beauty.

also lives in Barrie. He loves creating in his woodshop or kitchen. Jason is the proud father of five and grandfather of four.
He enjoys volunteering in many capacities, and being creative, Whatever he is doing, he likes to do it with his family.

Other Books by Tracey

Earwigs

Passion

.dance

Monica

Sleep: Snowflake Edition

Resurrect: As Above Edition

Other Books by Jason

Passion
She
About Face
Reaching
Journey Home
Sleep: Evergreen Edition – Seasons Collection
Ransom Notes: A Macabre Hypothesis
Reflections: not so subtle words
Resurrect: So Below Edition – Seasons Collection
Healing
Reality
An Angrier Man
The Diary of a Warrior
LOVElier Days
The Way Aliens Take Over
The Patreon Files: Volume 1
Things I May Say – From Time-to-Time
The Fools Journey
Beautiful Disaster
Fucking Our Way to Freedom
Shattered
Monsters In My Closet
A Crazier Man
My Public Downfall
Sickness
Filled with Magic
When Death Comes on a Tuesday
Imposter Syndrome
Chaos Reigns
All That Was Left Unsaid
Changes
In The Beginning: Anthology